HEAVY METAL

Heavy Metal

Bambery · Holdsworth
Kingsford-Smith

CADECO

HEAVY METAL
First published in 1994 by
George Bambery, Malcolm Holdsworth,
Robert Kingsford-Smith

Text and photographs ©
G. Bambery, M. Holdsworth, R. Kingsford-Smith

Enquiries should be addressed to the publisher at
116 Merrivale Lane, Turramurra NSW 2074, Australia

National Library of Australia
Cataloguing-in-Publication Data:

Bambery, G.
Heavy Metal

ISBN 0 646 18174 2.

1. Locomotives. 2. Railroad travel. 3. Locomotives —
Pictorial works. I. Holdsworth, Malcolm.
II. Kingsford-Smith, R. III. Title.

625.261

Designed and produced by
Deborah Brash/Brash Design Pty Ltd

Typeset by Post Typesetters, Brisbane
Printed in Singapore by Mandarin Offset

Photo page 1: Malcolm Holdsworth
Photo pages 2 and 3: Robert Kingsford-Smith
Photo page 6: George Bambery
Photos pages 8 and 9: Malcolm Holdsworth

CONTENTS

INTRODUCTION

· ·

HEAVY METAL is a world-ranging publication which displays the photographic work of three Australian steam locomotive enthusiasts: George Bambery, Malcolm Holdsworth and Robert Kingsford-Smith.

Left to right: *George Bambery, Malcolm Holdsworth, Robert Kingsford-Smith at the Grange Hotel, Witput, South Africa, 1978.*

Despite a combined total of over 75 years' photographic experience we have, until now, kept our light under a bushel, with only occasional contributions to other railfans' publications, three calendars and one joint book — *Famous Last Lines* to our credit. This can be attributed to typical railfan poverty. George has gained some visibility with previous work for Victorian Railways as a photojournalist.

We have divided the book into three parts, separately featuring the contributions of each photographer. The theme within the parts is not geographical; we have chosen to follow as much as possible a chronological order of photo selection which relates loosely

to our introductory comments. Subject matter includes action in Australia and in a significant number of other countries which operated steam from the early seventies onwards. The layout is intended to emphasise each photo by keeping down the number of secondary shots.

Why '*Heavy Metal*'? Well, these are some of our best photos and live steam is heavy in tonnage and sensory impact in real life. Also, if you imagine the weight of brass that we've put into the book, you will understand that the bank manager's attitude is not light either!

We hope you appreciate these images of our favourite industrial art form.

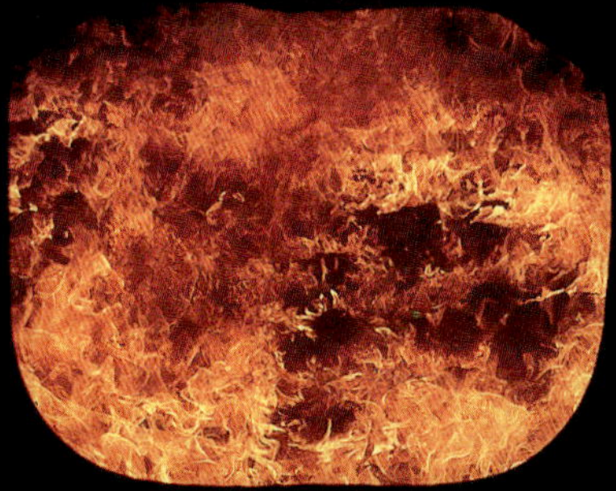

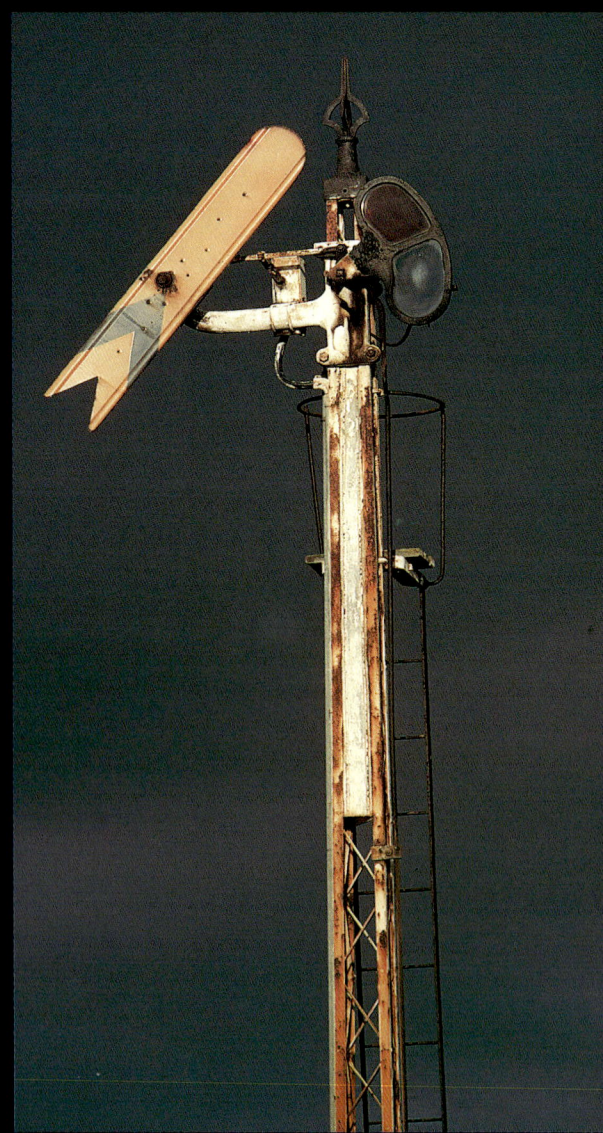

Heavy Metal

Chasing Dinosaurs

GEORGE BAMBERY

TRAINS HAVE ALWAYS BEEN A BIG PART OF MY LIFE. Growing up on my parents' farm at Rockbank, I'd look out over the rolling, treeless plains and watch them pass by. At night I'd hear them too, and tucked in my bed I'd lie and listen. I wondered where they were going, and always thought how exciting it would be to be the driver of such trains, charging through the night to unknown, far away places.

Back in those early years the trains that fascinated me were diesel-hauled. The Victorian Railways had a firm commitment to the General Motors salesman's catchcry: 'dieselise', and the long, interstate freights (known as Jets) on their western mainline had been well and truly placed in the hands of elegant, yet purposeful, blue and gold painted diesels.

Every lad has a hangout, a special place where time is spent during formative years, and mine became the local railway station. It was well within pedalling distance on my bicycle and several friendly stationmasters helped nurture my growing interest in railways. They patiently answered my incessant questions and I'd happily spend hours drawing pictures (trains of course), copying timetables or reading the railway's monthly 'Newsletter' magazine. All the while the big clock on the wall loudly marked the passing time. Telegraph bells tolled and clanged, levers were thrown and the trains roared on through.

Steam was pretty much alien to me then. Occasionally, however, the deep wail of a whistle was heard, and I'd be up our tankstand for a better view towards the railway. If I knew in advance that a steam loco was coming, by hook or by crook I'd be there to watch it. An old Kodak 'Brownie' which had been handed down to me was used to capture the moment (albeit not very well). The knowledge that steam was fast disappearing reinforced the need to record such events on film.

By joining several railway enthusiast societies I met other railfans and learnt that while steam was in its final hour in my

Saalfeld, East Germany 1980

home state, it faired considerably better elsewhere in the country, for example in New South Wales, where Australia's last regular steam workings would eventually occur.

School holidays in the early 1970s were spent around Broadmeadow Locomotive Depot in Newcastle. What a fantastic place — especially when you're only fifteen — not one, but two roundhouses crammed full of living, breathing steam locos. I'd live at the depot for days on end and cab-ride as many of the engines as possible. Number two roundhouse was where the hulking 60 Class Beyer-Garratts were stabled, and the deck of one of these roomy-cabbed machines was always a good spot to roll out the sleeping bag, but only after checking the roster to make sure the loco would be on shed until next morning.

Many's the time I've woken to the sound of kit bags sliding onto the footplate and exclamations from boiler suited men shining torches at me. Their words were usually along the lines of: 'What the hell have we got here?' Moments like these called for some fast talking: 'I'm a steam-starved Victorian up here on holidays from Melbourne; the chargeman said this one wasn't going out 'till six-thirty. Where are you fellas off to?'

'We're heading to Gosford on 668,' was the type of answer you wanted to hear, but it didn't really matter where they were going...

'Don't s'pose I could come along?'

The crews were super-friendly. More often than not you got a guernsey, and before long you'd be helping the fireman, and if lucky, maybe even the driver — as 260 tonnes of fire-breathing monster wheeled headlong into a pastelled dawn.

Such are my best memories of the New South Wales Railways; indeed of my teenage years. However, my obsession with playing 'boy fireman' meant I didn't get many lineside photos, and being too young to drive a car didn't help either. Government steam operations ceased in early 1973.

That year I finished school and at the beginning of 1974 I began studying Agricultural Economics at the University of New England. Because of my addiction to steam, my final few years of secondary study had been rather unsettled, but now my parents had every reason to expect that I would settle down to some serious career-building activities. University was lots of fun, and I did well in the first term exams, but something was missing. I knew that over 2,500 steam locomotives were still running in South Africa. Some fellow enthusiasts had gone over there to work as firemen, and the more I heard about this steamy paradise, the more I wanted to be there.

Imagine my folks' surprise when I arrived home unexpectedly at the end of April and announced that I had deferred my studies and was going to South Africa to fire steam locomotives!

They eventually accepted the idea, and I worked at several jobs to scrape an airfare and some travellers cheques together. A couple of weeks after my nineteenth birthday I parked my fading blue denims on the seat of a Qantas 707 as far as Johannesburg. I'd also just purchased a Pentax Spotmatic F SLR — a real camera at last — along with a 200mm lens, and I was eager to start taking the type of shots I'd previously only dreamed of.

'See you around Christmas' were my parting words to Mum and Dad. Luckily I didn't say which Christmas: it would be eighteen months before I eventually returned.

I photographed steam throughout southern Africa, and then worked as a fireman on SAR at Sydenham depot in Port Elizabeth. My training was with top link driver Chris Botha, and I experienced the thrill of being on highly polished Pacifics as they accelerated Uitenhage suburban trains up to 100kph between stations. Despite the joy of working on steam and fulfilling a childhood dream, it was hard going. Shifts were long and the deep fireboxes of most South African engines required plenty of shovelling.

Having passed as a fireman it would normally have been straight on to the shunts in the busy yards of New Brighton or PE harbour, except I'd managed to arrange a swap and went on relief to Grahamstown. Although there was no motive power variety at this depot there was plenty of road working. Most runs were to Alicedale and while slogging up the long steep grades from here on 19D 4-8-2s I really learnt how to fire.

When I returned to Sydenham I had my fair share of shunts, but also scored some road jobs to Klipplaat on the Hendrie-designed 15ARs. Although these locos were free steamers the outward journey up the escarpment was pretty tough. It would take around 12 hours to get there and by the time you booked off you had usually shovelled more than 13 tonnes of coal. Fortunately the return run was mainly downhill.

By March 1975 it was time to move on. My air ticket was through to London and I was determined to use at least half of it before its validity ran out. I wanted to photograph the last steam workings in Europe, particularly the West German 012 Pacifics on the Rheine–Emden line before their scheduled withdrawal with the introduction of the Deutsche Bundesbahn's summer timetable. Seeing these fat-stacked oil burners working expresses tabled for 130kph running compensated for not staying longer at Sydenham.

Other 'gems' in Europe at that stage were the Portuguese steamers of considerable antiquity which worked Porto suburban services and the main and branch lines in the Douro Valley. Behind the 'Iron Curtain' in Eastern Europe steam could also still be found in abundance, although cloak and dagger photographic techniques were usually required to reduce the risk of arrest and inevitable film confiscation. Until the early 1980s information about railways was considered to be of strategic importance in Eastern Bloc countries, despite the development of all-knowing satellite intelligence systems in the West.

By the northern hemisphere winter of 1975 I had scraped up enough cash to get me home via Japan. I'd always dreamed of photographing main line steam in heavy snow, and on the northern island of Hokkaido JNR's last steam workings were about to finish. I was somewhat put out when it turned out to be a late winter, and at the end of my stay on a fixed excursion airfare from Bangkok, the snows had yet to arrive.

I returned to Bangkok to find that a visa mix-up would prevent me photographing steam in southern Thailand. I was only allowed entry on a transit visa, which meant I could not overland it to Singapore as planned. I decided to spend the time originally intended for Thailand back in Japan, so with the last of my cash I bought another 10 day excursion to Tokyo. By now the snow was falling, but a five day rail strike was called the day after I arrived! Despite all the traumas I eventually got some snow shots and managed to be home in time for Christmas.

Back in Australia I realised that the travel bug had bitten me. In July 1976 I again set off in search of steam on an overland journey to Europe. My travels came to an abrupt halt in Calcutta; I'd contracted hepatitis while in Burma. Six weeks later I was strong enough to travel again, and pushed on. I was determined to get to Turkey and take shots of the 'Skyliners' on the spectacular Zonguldak line before they finished.

By the time I arrived in Damascus in Syria I needed a car. Getting the shots on foot was proving to be a real drag, particularly since I hadn't completely recovered from the illness. The Stationmaster at Damascus spoke English and invited me to stay at his place. When I mentioned my transportation dilemma he said: 'There is a place. Tomorrow we will go there'.

On arrival the place wasn't quite what I had expected. As far as the eye could see there were shiny luxury vehicles — Mercedes, Jaguars, BMWs, Rolls Royces — anything your average oil sheik could ask for. 'This place is not for me,' I told my host. 'I need an old, inexpensive car. Let's go.'

'Wait. We will see,' he countered and strode purposefully over to a group of loitering salesmen. There was much head shaking amongst the huddle of men that quickly formed, but after some time one of the new arrivals began pointing to the back of the huge, sandy car-lot.

We worked our way to the back corner where an old, dust-covered Volkswagen Beetle was parked. Investigation showed that it was pretty much complete, but would it go? A battery appeared and was installed amidst growing excitement. To the delight of us all the motor roared to life after a few turns of the starter. I was invited to go for a spin and did so — with all the kids who had assembled to watch also climbing aboard. Apart from a bent front axle the old girl was in pretty good shape, so negotiations began. Eventually the figure became realistic and we finally settled on US$300.

From Damascus that Volksie and I headed to Amman in Jordan, then back through Syria to Turkey and eventually across the Eastern bloc. The stories of these travels could fill a book on their own, but the main thing was to be able to get to photographic locations relatively easily (despite blizzards, icy roads and maniac bus drivers). Fortunately Allah was on my side and some of the resulting photos remain my most treasured images.

Once more in Australia, I decided photography should be my vocation and began studying part-time for a Bachelor of Arts in Photography at the Royal Melbourne Institute of Technology. In 1979 I was lucky enough to get a job with the then Victorian Railways as a photographer. Overseas travel in search of steam continued whenever possible, and many of these trips were with Sydneysider Robert (Rags) Kingsford-Smith, who I had met in South Africa back in 1974.

Rags and I have covered a lot of the world together. Looking back on some of those early travels we were a pretty formidable duo. We'd set off on meticulously planned journeys with round-world airline tickets that bulged with an amazing number of stop-overs, each designed to land us in a major city closest to which steam was still working. Such trips were crammed into our annual vacations, and generally a couple of weeks leave without pay were also wangled.

We lived to tell the tale of numerous arrests as suspected spies or terrorists, escaped impending wars, traversed seemingly impassable roads and survived climatic conditions ranging from debilitating heat to freezing blizzards. We had scarce time to ponder such obstacles; the pressure was always on to get someplace or other before another member of the steam species became extinct.

Malcolm Holdsworth became a starter on trips in more recent years, and the three of us became a team, always aspiring to two golden rules: Get the shots . . . and live to see them.

Now that steam has gone from most corners of the planet there's finally a chance to pause for breath and reflect. *Heavy Metal* is the result.

Australia, October 1970 Dusk is well advanced as R761 waits for departure at Bendigo with an enthusiasts' special. Soon this high-drivered Hudson will be rolling towards Melbourne, and as the grades of the Great Dividing Range are tackled, all and sundry will once more recall the raw power of mainline steam in action.

South Africa, August 1974 GF Class double Pacific Garratt 2417 lays a trail of steam over the winter-brown countryside near Creighton as it works the Pietermaritzburg to Franklin pick up.

Portugal, May 1975 The Porto narrow gauge system was a
joy to behold, with a stable of 40 to 90 year-old locomotives
of 2–6–0, 2–8–2 and 0–4–4–0 wheel arrangements. In this
scene sprightly 70 year old 2–6–0 tank E114 departs Avenida
da Franca with a passenger consist for Senhora da Hora,
including a beautifully varnished wooden-bodied car.

Portugal, May 1975 Trackwork was being done the old fashioned way at Régua while an inside cylindered 'B12' 5'6" gauge 4–6–0 kicked wagons around the yard.

Portugal, May 1975 At Régua Station a 2–4–6–0 Mallet tank awaits departure time with an evening service to Villa Real. Featuring copper-capped chimneys and large oil lamps, these interestingly-wheeled metre gauge locomotives graced two of the branches off the main Douro Valley line until the end of the seventies.

CELLATRON

BERLIN OSTBAHNHOF

AUSGANG

← AUSGANG →
← ÜBERGANG ZUR S-BAHN →
S-BAHN FAHRKARTEN
← FERN- U. PLATZKARTEN AUSKUNFT.
BANK WECHSELSTELLE
DEUTSCHES ROTES KREUZ über die STRASSE

East Germany, August 1975 Train photography in the DDR was definitely 'verboten' at this time, so cloak and dagger techniques were successfully applied for this late afternoon study of the Berlin Ostbahnhof

Thailand, November 1975 Steam in a significant place.
The Burma Railway was built with the blood, sweat and tears
of Australian and British POWs during the Japanese
occupation of Thailand in the Second World War. Over
thirty years later Japanese built C 56 705 was silhouetted on
the bridge over the River Kwai with the 06.00 Kanchanaburi
to Nam Tok mixed.

Japan, November 1975 Swirling cats' tails gleam in the late sun as a D51 storms upgrade with coal from the Yubari mines near Kawabata.

Japan, December 1975
Smoke fills the valley as D51
1086 starts train number
5795 past the snow covered
water tank at Momijiyama.
Less than two months later
steam had finished working
on the JNR.

▲ **Japan, November 1975** The northern island of Hokkaido was the last bastion of JNR steam operations. On the mainline between Shigashi Muroran and Iwamizawa a D51 rolls through Shibun with a southbound freight.

◄ **Japan, October 1975** Autumn tints the foliage as another Mikado makes time on goods service near Shiraoi.

▶ **Syria, November 1976** The ruins of an ancient Roman amphitheatre at Bosra frame a Borsig-built 2–8–0 which has just cut off the passenger service from Deraa.

▼ **Syria, November 1976** Next morning at 06.45 the train returned from Bosra to Deraa.

**◄ Turkey,
December 1976**
Turkish delights.

**▼ Turkey,
December 1976**
46106, a Robert
Stephenson-built 2–8–2,
departs Turan on a
suburban working from
Izmir to Ciyli.

▲ **Turkey, November 1977** Mosques, mountains and
motive power. Corpet Louvet 2–10–0 56917 pilots a
Kriegslok away from the Crusaders' fort at Seljuk.

◄ **Turkey, December 1976** The pastel tones of Izmiri
suburbia dot the hillsides as an ageing French-built 2–10–0
heads another suburban service out of Hilal.

Jugoslavia, January 1977 A four cylindered 01 Class
2–6–2 lays out a long steam-trail in this winter scene as it
works the 13.35 Kraljevo to Lapovo passenger.

Turkey, December 1976 'Skyliner' at dusk. Vulcan of Wilkes Barre built these impressive, semi-streamlined 2–10–0s for the TCDD, and members of the class had carte blanche on Zonguldak line services until diesels displaced them in the late seventies. This one was heading north on the long climb past the village of Kurşunlu.

▲ **Turkey, December 1976** Action on the horseshoes above Çamlibel. A Samsun-bound standard 2–10–0 blasts clear of a snowshed in full cry.

◄ **Turkey, January 1977** New Year's day at Sumuçak. The 'Skyliner' 2–10–0 based at this remote station for banking duties has had its fire cleaned, and awaits its next call for helper service on the steeply graded Zonguldak line in Turkey's rugged north-west. Villagers are on hand to collect any skerricks of unburnt coal, which they'll use for cooking or helping to heat their homes during the long, cold winter.

◀ Turkey, February 1984
Marker lights push back the fog at Kavak as a 2–8–0 waits to cross an opposing movement. The TCDD used the former Prussian State railways as a rich source of locomotives. The German builder Nohab constructed these 2–8–0s to the Prussian G8.2 design.

▶ India, January 1983
The Taj Mahal is an awesome experience at any time of day.

▼ India, October 1976 WP7003 departs New Delhi with the 07.15 'Taj Express' to Agra.

Indonesia, August 1976 One of the most photogenic
roundhouses on the planet stands at Tebing Tinggi in
Sumatra. A 2–8–4 well tank built by Werkspoor in 1916
graces the turntable in this tropical setting.

▲ **Kenya, November 1977**
Mt. Kilimanjaro lurks under
Equatorial afternoon clouds
and oil-smoke from 6007
returning to Voi on the
Taveta mixed.

◄ **Kenya, November 1977**
Friends you meet.

Turkey, December 1976 'Heavy metal'. This chunky S160 Class 2–8–0 is ready for business as it starts out of Karabuk to begin its shift shunting the nearby steelworks and factories.

Turkey, December 1976 An ex Prussian G8 0–8–0
approaches Buca with the 07.05 service from Izmir's
Alsançak Station.

▲ **Jugoslavia, January 1977** Sometimes you just get lucky. This 51 Class 2–6–2T was caught working the 15.52 service to Gorna Stubica.

▶ **East Germany, December 1977** Winter has really taken hold of the Cranzahl–Oberwiesenthal line and the stillness is momentarily broken as a 2–10–2T skirts along the Czechoslovakian border.

Bolivia, January 1978 High on the Bolivian altiplano
Baldwin 2–10–2 No.706 slogs upgrade across a fine stone
viaduct towards Villazon with a freight from Tupiza.

Brazil, December 1977 'The driver'. Without doubt the noisiest cab ride I've ever experienced: the man with the throttle was intent on making 2–8–0 No. 68 buck along the 750mm gauge towards São João del Rei as fast as it could.

Bolivia, January 1978 Hitachi 2–8–2 No. 663 is high
in the Andes near Betanzos with the weekly train between
Potosi and Sucre.

▲ Bolivia, February 1978 Sister Mikado No. 666 pounds its way towards the summit of the Condor Pass. Roof riding passengers may have missed out on a seat but they had a hell of a view.

◄ Bolivia, February 1978 At Carlos Machicao — as with every other village along the way — the arrival of the daily train to Rio Mulatos was greeted with much interest, as it was the only communication with the outside world.

Brazil, January 1978 Metre gauge 2–10–4 No. 308 gets 2,000 tonnes of coal moving up the yard at Criciuma on the Dona Teresa Cristina system in Santa Catarina province. Once wound up, the big Texas type locos would move the trains with ease at 80kph.

Chile, January 1978 Baldwin 0–6–0T No. 487
whiles away the idle hours at Temuco shed.

Indonesia, May 1980 No-one will ever repeat this photo.
In addition to the absence of steam, Mount Galunggung
erupted and shortened itself considerably some years after
this shot was taken of the Tjikadjang train returning to
Tjibatu behind the sole remaining CC 10 Mallet tank.

Hungary, May 1980 A tracery of branches frames
this silhouette of 375.552 on an evening passenger near
Abaujszanto, between Hidasnemeti and Szerencs.

▲ **East Germany, May 1980** Track work is suspended to allow the passage of this Saalfeld-based 44 Class.

▶ **Austria, May 1980** The driver of this 0–8–0 on the Gmünd narrow gauge system continues his oiling despite unseasonal flurries of snow.

East Germany, May 1980 A 44 Class 2–10–0 trundles
along the Saal valley with general goods loading for Jena.

Chile, February 1982 The morning train from
Lonquimay to Victoria approaches Malalcuelo.

Turkey, February 1984 Rural solitude is briefly
disturbed on the climb between Kavak and Ladik.

Turkey, January 1982 The Tatvan posta heads east towards
the mountains beyond Elazig in ethnically tense Kurdistan.

Pakistan, January 1984 The once weekly mixed from
Bostan to Zhob climbs between Khanhai and Zarghun in
immaculate late afternoon light. A rare feature of this narrow
gauge service was the provision of a sleeping car. Although
there was some risk in chasing trains on the unstable
Pakistani northwest frontier, the rewards in terms of scenery
and steam made it all worthwhile. The superb lamb dinners
at night also went some way to easing the day's tensions.

Pakistan, January 1984 Three days later, and 24 hours behind schedule, the return working from Zhob reaches the freezing precincts of Khanmetazai.

▲ **Pakistan, January 1984** The train from Quetta to Chaman, on the Afghan border, is dwarfed by the peaks of the Hindu Kush as it ventures beyond Bostan in Baluchistan.

◄ **Pakistan, January 1984** Space is precious on all Pakistani trains. Even HGS 2299's buffer beam was utilised at Bostan.

Pakistan, January 1984 Cloud shrouds the ranges in the
background as an HGS Class 2–8–0 barks uphill towards
Shellabagh at the summit of Kojak Pass. A sister machine,
banking the train from behind, was further back around
the corner.

▲ China, January 1992
In possibly the world's last
great surviving steam show a
QJ 2–10–2 climbs above Men Jia
Wan with the Beijing–Lanzhou
passenger.

◄ China, January 1992
Gentle people of the north.

▲ China, January 1992
Double 2–10–2s assault the grades west of Zhongwei in a steady procession. Big power, big tonnage and sometimes blistering cold hold attraction for railfans of all nationalities.

◄ China, January 1992
Even Bactrian camels feel cold when it's twenty below.

China, January 1992 'Ice sculpture'.

Reflections at 52 Degrees South

MALCOLM HOLDSWORTH

AT THE TIME OF WRITING IT IS DARK AND I'M hunched before a feeble coal fire in the tiny hotel at Bella Vista. The latitude is 52 degrees south; a 750 mm gauge railway runs by only 100 metres from the front door; the country cannot be other than Argentina and the fire is losing its struggle with the –18 degree centigrade exterior temperature. Motive power on the infrequent coal trains which pass outside the hotel is steam . . .

My earliest memories of steam are of a handful of occasions when my father took me to the railway station at Hornsby in suburban Sydney to watch the evening expresses go north. In the late 1950s steam still dominated these trains and the job of engine driver was much admired. With their hats, ties and dustcoats, the top roster enginemen sat impossibly high above the platforms while my infant ears recoiled from the blast of whistles, the scream of safety valves and the crash of locomotive exhausts.

The engines were much larger then. Climbing into the cab of even a humble standard goods shunter brought on sensory overload and when calloused hands passed me back down to Dad I felt relief from the fear of potent forces. But the magic stuck.

The passage of time saw steam replaced in New South Wales at about the same rate that my ability to photograph it on the move increased. From 1968 onwards I spent weekends and holidays camping trackside with other railfans to see the last of the 'big show' on the Short North line between Gosford and Newcastle. As we drove north on Friday nights, we found ourselves listening to a tune which almost became an anthem: The Hollies' 'He ain't Heavy, He's my Brother'. In those days the hulking 60 Class Beyer Garratts ruled the drag freight traffic,

Townsville, Queensland 1960

while smooth-barrelled 38 Class Pacifics heralded the approach of Newcastle Flyers with clipped stack talk and melodious chimes.

My photographic career started with a Braun fixed lens automatic 127 camera. Although relatively foolproof for its time, the fastest shutter speed of a hundredth of a second did amazing things to the buffer beams of fast moving Pacifics. A Yashika YL, also fixed lens but 35mm, came my way for Christmas 1969. Expresses could now be stopped, but a bizarre preference for poor film types and an incomprehensible need to get 38 shots off a roll cost me dearly in lost coverage.

A feeling first sensed in Australia and borne out in my overseas travels is that of always being too late. No matter where I have pursued my hobby, the most scenic lines have nearly always gone diesel or closed. If steam is still operating, the more interesting locomotive types have usually been retired. From discussion with those of my peers who lost their parochial outlook earlier than I, there is little comfort in knowing that they too carry the albatrosses of lost opportunity around their necks together with their Nikons and Pentaxes.

Like most people I work for a living full-time and am only able to chase steam during my holidays. Nevertheless, this external focus has stood me in good stead throughout the ebb and flow of personal relationships and career strife.

Many consider steam enthusiasm to be backward looking, and most fans have a large nostalgic streak in their makeup, but I take the view that the photographic activity is a pursuit of excellence. This may at first seem rather pretentious, but I did say a pursuit of excellence: attaining it is another matter entirely. Even after all these years I still have no problem stuffing up a simple standard three-quarter shot. I am consoled by an oft-stated observation of that great South African photographer, Charlie Lewis: 'Hell man, I still haven't taken the perfect shot!'. If he hasn't with his wealth of brilliant images, then who am I to worry?

Heavy Metal has been on my mind, as it were, for some years now and I take great pleasure in joining two of my best mates, George Bambery and Robert Kingsford-Smith as co-creators. Any comparison on the basis of artistic merit between their contributions and my own leaves me suitably humbled.

Everyone who has pursued interests away from his homeland knows that pitfalls of ignorance of local custom and physical difficulty lie in the path of even the simplest objectives. During a campervan tour of Eastern Europe in 1974 the illogic of official attitudes was brought home to me most forcefully.

While hiding beside the Berlin–Dresden main line to photograph 01.2 and 01.05 Class Pacifics on the morning expresses, my companions and I were accosted by a portly village policeman on a bicycle who warned us that photography was 'verboten'. After he departed, but before we could disregard his instructions, we were more forcefully cautioned by a thin and angry member of the Volkspolizei on a three horsepower scooter.

Despite a change of location to a branch line in the area, and with a double-headed goods in our viewfinders, we were nabbed by the driver of a squad car and promptly escorted to Elsterwerda Station. Here the signalman's protests were stifled when our uniformed benefactor emerged from under the station awning and invited us to shoot as many trains as we liked. Photography at stations was legal!

Somewhat unnerved by all this official attention we moved to Poland. Arriving at Zagan the next day, and now understanding the 'rules of engagement' in communist Europe, five of us sallied forth onto the platforms amid panting Ok1 4–6–0s and O149 2–6–2s and started blazing away in all directions. Scant minutes later we were overtaken by the hostile word 'Apparat!' and turned to confront a five foot tall chimpanzee in uniform toting an enormous handgun. He was soon weighed down by about a dozen cameras as well.

A raincoated Russian finally turned up late in the afternoon and invited us from our cells in the town's police station for a chat. The essence of his message was that photography was permitted in the countryside but definitely not at stations or other militarily sensitive areas like bridges and junctions. Needless to say the exposed film confiscated from our cameras featured some pleasant open-fields coverage of high speed Pacifics on the Berlin–Dresden expresses.

Australia, August 1972 Steam's last gasp in New South Wales featured combinations of locomotives on the Short North line from Gosford to Newcastle which had not been seen for years. Thanks to the oil strike, 2-8-0 Standard Goods 5412 and a 59 Class Baldwin 2-8-2 lock couplers with 700 tons of goods in the back platform at Gosford Station.

Far eclipsing these and other trials are my fondest memories of steam in action — dropping into blackberries at Hawkmount on New South Wales's Sydney–Newcastle line at 4.00am from a slow moving green 3813 on 19 North (not a comfortable sensation, but you had to be there to hear the 'Eighter' restart the train); eating wurst and drinking beer at 156kph behind 012 075 on a Rheine–Norddeich boat train; listening to a pair of GMAs surround me and then double back on themselves on my first visit to City View on Natal's Greytown line and photographing the sinuous progress of the toy train towards Darjeeling.

How could I leave out the deafening Kraankuil nightscape as a 25NC accelerated uphill from Orange River with the 800 tonne Trans Karoo Express; or Vordernberg with its winter-white slopes; or the bustle of ancient power at Porto's Trindade terminus; or the vast emptiness of Patagonia's Esquel line? While memories are specific to each individual, steam fans have in common a bond with their subject matter most akin to that of hunter and prey.

It is a measure of the decline of steam that it no longer moves people and produce at the heart of the developed world. It has even ceased to belch the atmosphere into Gosford, Bloemfontein, Pamplona and Saalfeld Stations. The most evocative of its rural haunts resound to the chant of diesel or whine of electric traction. Hawkmount, the Douro Valley, Sir Lowry's Pass, Rheine–Emden and Kimberley–De Aar read like an honour roll of battles lost. Most succumbed years ago . . .

So I sit at latitude 52 degrees south. The end of the earth. The fire is nearly out — a last smoky breath . . .

Hang on! Was that a whistle?

▲ **South Africa, August 1974** One of the most
photographed locations on the Kroonstad–Bloemfontein line
in the Orange Free State was the dam at Glen. The still
waters reflected the daily passing of a procession of trains
hauled by big Mountains until March 1976. Last light finds a
15F northbound on one such working.

◀ **Australia, February 1971** Fire and rain. At nearly eighty
years of age, veteran 4–6–0 3246 looks none too happy
about getting her feet wet. However, marks on the walls of
the station at Maitland, New South Wales attest to a history
of major flooding compared to which Mother Nature had
barely turned on the tap this time. Needless to say, the
afternoon 'boat train' to Singleton berthed at its destination
none the worse for wear.

◄ **South Africa, August 1974** Natal Province was a treasure trove of Garratt power with no less than five classes still working on the 3'6" in mid-1974. Splendid scenery, winter steam effects, legendary meals and hospitable publicans made it a joy to motorcade. None of those redeeming features is evident here as a GF 4–6–2+2–6–4 leads the Matatiele passenger into the gathering dusk.

▶ **South Africa, August 1974** My friends and I had arrived in the dead of night and set up camp in the centre of the bottom horseshoe at City View on the Pietermaritzburg–Greytown line. The imminent end of steam was brought home to us when the first two downhill trains showed up behind diesels. After dawn all was steam, including this bunker first GMA.

Austria, October 1974 Austria is famous for its mountain
scenery, which is enhanced in autumn by the colouring of the
leaves and early snowfalls. Somewhat less remarkable by
1974 was the range of steam motive power left operating on
the ÖBB, where freight duties were almost entirely
performed by ageing Kriegslok war locomotives. Julie
Andrews was nowhere in sight as a 52 Class 2–10–0 slogged
north between Klaus and Linz on a block load of limestone.

Austria, October 1974 A 52 Class awaits the right of way at Summerau on the Czechoslovak border as the sun fades on the horizon.

Italy, October 1974 Franco Crosti boilered 741 Class 2–8–0
number 320 bursts from a tunnel near Vandoies on the
Fortezza–San Candido line in the Dolomite Region. Sporting
a wheel arrangement that is more synonymous with slog than
speed, these noisy engines could really turn it on when
working the passenger in the hands of a flamboyant latin.

Switzerland, September 1974 The Brienz Rothorn Bahn near Interlaken operates a steam rack service throughout the summer months each year. Its main revenue comes from holiday makers who are often transported into song by the alpine vistas and fragrant air. A quieter cargo, sourced to the herds of contented dairy cows which dot the mountain slopes, is loaded at a wayside halt.

Spain, November 1974 The lead 141F 2–8–2 of a banked
goods train rests in Pamplona Station before tackling the
grades to the north of town.

Spain, November 1974 The soft colours of a late autumn afternoon surround a 141F ambling its all stations passenger along level track between Alsasua and Pamplona.

Portugal, November 1974 The broad gauge railway paralleling the Douro Valley upstream from Régua in the wine growing region of northern Portugal played host to outside cylinder and inside cylinder Henschel 4–6–0s as well as a lesser number of 2–8–0s in the mid-1970s. Here an inside cylinder Ten Wheeler crosses the river at Ferradossa. Below shows the cab detail of an outside cylinder 4–6–0.

Rhodesia, January 1975 The sun's searchlight bounces off the flanks of 15th Class Hudson Garratt 394 as it drops downhill with the then Rhodesian Railways' Bulawayo–Gwelo afternoon mixed. The 15ths are the most nicely proportioned Garratts I have seen and they are capable of 100kph, when pushed, on passenger duties. More importantly, at the time of writing many of these delightful locomotives are still in regular service. So is the superb fauna.

South Africa, March 1975
The Hottentots Hollands Mountains loom over a labouring GEA on Sir Lowry's Pass. At this late date many Capetown crews were getting few steam turns and thus were losing a certain amount of physical condition. It was not unknown for a railfan to jump out of a chasing car and climb into the labouring engine to shovel up the uncompensated 1 in 40s.

▲ **South Africa, March 1975** Heavy metal indeed! A 14CRB and GEA pour on maximum traction as they restart a freight from Sir Lowry's Pass Station. When overnighting in this stunning area, aromatic firewood from the gum trees, great slabs of beef from the Elgin butcher's shop, jacket potatoes, a nice Stellenbosch red and live stereo steam combined to promote a feeling of well-being in everyone taking part.

◄ **South Africa, March 1975** GEA Garratt 4041 has rolled its load of empty bogie fruit vans into the still heat of Sir Lowry's Pass Station and now receives attention from its crew and the coal trimmers. The hard part comes soon for the fireman of this large hand-fired 4–8–2+2–8–4.

▲ **Germany, April 1975** The Ruhr industrial area has an enormous appetite for motive power. The hunger is somewhat reduced on Saturday afternoons, when this group of three cylinder 44 Class 2–10–0s rested their springs at Gelsenkirchen Bismarck shed.

▶ **Italy, April 1975** A 741 Class Franco Crosti cools its heels at the engine servicing point in San Candido yard before the trip back to Fortezza.

Germany, December 1974 With their drumming oil fires, fat stacks, two metre drivers and superb three cylinder beat, the 012 Class Pacifics stationed at Rheine near the Dutch border were complete masters of their roster. Here 012 080 thrashes south along the superb trackwork at Lathen with a D schnellzug.

Germany, April 1975 The 012s were within months of finishing when I arrived there for a lightning second visit in 1975. These machines had mightily impressed this Pacific-starved Australian the previous year with feats such as the near 160kph run on the Norddeich boat train mentioned in my introduction.

Australia, September 1976 Now let's be honest, would the kids have ridden this far for a diesel? South Maitland Railways' 2–8–2 tank Number 26 rolls over Swamp Creek Bridge, Abermain in the lower Hunter Valley of New South Wales.

Australia, September 1975 J&A Brown's Kitson 2–8–2T
Number 9 pauses at the end of the Hexham coal washing
plant in the lower Hunter Valley before running around its
load of non-aired wagons. The mood is yellow.

South Africa, August 1978 As steam silhouettes the hillside a GMA Garratt stamps upgrade near Topping on the Montagu Pass in Cape Province. In an area where baboons are frequently sighted, and leopards are not rare, even the auto stoker-fired 4–8–2+2–8–4s could struggle in bad weather. A sigh of relief no doubt accompanied every successful climb.

South Africa, August 1978 Sunrise catches a 3321 series 19D blowing down at a wayside halt near Le Roux at the head of 8 up Port Elizabeth to Capetown passenger.

South Africa, August 1978 A 19D plus 15AR double header races 42006 passenger into the gloom near Teebus on the Rosmead–Stormberg line.

Poland, April 1980 The Astoria Hotel lies on the outskirts of Klodzko. The Poles have not always been as relaxed about unsanctioned steam photography as they now are. The Astoria had a window overlooking the main line south to the Czech border. The window opened and a telephoto lens cranked out to capture a TY2 Class 2–10–0 in the mist. The culprit got away.

▲ **Austria, April 1980** In a time-honoured ritual, 399.02 and 298.207 race their mixed trains out of Alt Nagelberg as light snow swirls about. The Gmünd 750mm system, on Austria's north-eastern border with Czechoslovakia, is an anachronism which runs to this day, albeit with diesel except for some passenger services in the summer months.

▶ **Indonesia, July 1983** Oil burning 4–4–0 B5138 lays a smokescreen over the Javan jungle as it accelerates the morning Labuan–Rangkasbitung passenger high above fast-flowing tropical waters. Within days yours truly was immobilised by dysentery and then glandular fever which lasted for some months.

East Germany, April 1980 The area around Saalfeld is quite rustic, being graced by meandering rivers, small villages and green fields. There is a nice little climb just out of town to test Gera bound engines before they have really warmed to the task. The rakish lines of a Deutsche Reichsbahn 01.05 Pacific are partly hidden by salmon-tinged steam as it heels into a corner on the hill.

▲ Pakistan, January 1987
SPS Class inside cylinder 4–4–0
power races an evening stopper
away from Sargodha in what
would have been familiar style
all round the British Empire a
hundred years earlier.

◄ Pakistan, January 1987
A playful bear applauds the
departure of a 4–4–0 near
Wilsonpore.

▲ **Pakistan, January 1987**
The winter wind carries a chill
which prospective passengers
on the Mari Indus 750mm gauge
system do well to respect.

◄ **Pakistan, January 1987**
The porter at Mari Indus
Station prepares for some
heavy lifting.

India, December 1986
The Kurseong workers' train climbs energetically near Tung on its way to the summit of the Darjeeling line.

▲ Australia, August 1987 Pretty scenes like this are amazingly fragile. Within a month the railway operations at J&A Brown's Stockrington Colliery had fallen in the face of the road imperative. If you look closely at the smokebox you'll realise that the 10 Class 2–8–2 tank wasn't rapt about its prospects either.

▶ Australia, August 1987 The brake gear inside this four wheeled van once kept the Hunter Valley's non-aired coal trains safe.

◀ Australia, September 1979 Tour engine 3102, a 4–6–0 converted by its former government owner from a 4–6–4 tank, pauses in the roundhouse at Goulburn, New South Wales before rolling down to the station to pick up its train.

Ecuador, June 1989 Washaways had split the Guayaquil and Quito Railway between Alausi and Riobamba in the late 1970s. The line from the coast to Alausi, including the famous 'Devil's Nose' reverses, still saw steam in the form of chunky American 2–8–0s. These worked on the daily mixed trains, climbing through near-vertical equatorial scenery. Here a loco slumbers through the night before its morning run back to the coast.

Argentina, July 1990 Occasionally one tires of allowing engine and train to fill the whole frame. Of course the scenery on the Esquel line does tend to put these things into proper perspective.

▲ **Argentina, July 1989** Hitachi 2–10–2 Number 104 waits for a cross at Bella Vista on the Rio Gallegos line. The sunset goes on and on and the subtle changes in sky colour stretch even the most fertile imagination.

◄ **Australia, March 1988** Sunrise does strange things to the snout of a 'Pig'. 3642, a 4–6–0 of the former New South Wales Government Railways, was engaged in tour service for the Australian Bicentennial celebrations near Orange in the central west of the state.

Argentina, July 1992 In what was my least successful foray
overseas in recent years, Argentina turned on freezing
conditions, work attitudes by railwaymen approaching that
of an informal strike, airports closed by snow and a really
lousy exchange rate. At least the unpredictability of the last
was normal. At Rio Gallegos the elements seemed
determined to deny us a moving locomotive.

Argentina, July 1989 At latitude 52 degrees south. The
end of the earth. It's cold here and although there is some
acceptable scenery, the incredible sky makes it compelling
silhouette territory. Here a Japanese built, mechanically
stokered 2–10–2 climbs above Bella Vista inbound for Rio
Gallegos with 1,200 tonnes of coal. Not bad for 750mm gauge.

▲ **South Africa, July 1991** A newly risen sun catches the vapour trail of a low flying 25NC near Modder River on the Kimberley–De Aar line.

◄ **South Africa, August 1991** Aquatic cattle pay no attention to the Knysna–George mixed near Sedgefield, Cape Province.

▲ **Germany, January 1993** During January 1993 we were blessed with eleven days of clear sky. In earlier years I had spent two separate weeks in the Harz Mountains for a total of one hour's sunshine. A 2–10–2T drapes the countryside with steam as it climbs between Stiege and Hasselfelde.

▲ **Germany, January 1993** Light loading is a feature of the Gernrode metre gauge system and the big 2–10–2 tank is doing it easy in the snow west of Stiege.

◀ **Germany, January 1993** They do wonderful things with the time in Europe in winter. It's already after 9.00am and Meyer 99.712 extends the dawn with the first train of empties for the kaolin mine on the Oschatz–Mügeln narrow gauge line.

China, January 1994 Shortly after sunrise Double QJs pit
a combined 6,000 horsepower against the 1 in 80 grades of
Men Jia Wan.

China, January 1994 Winter temperatures at Men Jia Wan on the edge of the Gobi Desert can be brutal. Not so on this occasion as a QJ Class 2–10–2 canters upgrade with a stopping passenger in a relatively benign minus 5 degrees C.

▲ **Zimbabwe, July 1993** A 15th Class and 20th Class snooze in the early sun at Bulawayo Loco. Up until May 1993 shed boss David Putnam had to juggle over 70 working engines of four different classes and wheel arrangements. The diminutive double 2–6–2 14th Class, lanky 15th Class double Hudsons and 16th Class double 2–8–2s shared roads with the giant 4–8–2+2–8–4 20th Class.

◄ **Zimbabwe, July 1993** The fireman and assistant fireman of Garratt 424 have got time for a break as they sit in Thomson Junction Station with train number 129 from Victoria Falls.

India, January 1993 Machinery of motion — detail of the double sets of Walschaert's valve gear on a Nilgiri rack tank engine.

Zimbabwe, July 1993 The sudden collapse of steam main
line working in May 1993 came as a real shock. Fortunately
balance goods workings were required for several rail tours.
A 15th Class-headed empty oil train hits dawn outside
Bulawayo, bound for Plumtree.

Zimbabwe, July 1993 A 15th struggles to overcome inertia and sticking brakes as it starts a Plumtree goods working out of Westgate yard.

Steam, Steaks and Stars

ROBERT KINGSFORD-SMITH

FAMILY HOLIDAYS IN MY EARLIEST YEARS WERE spent in the Blue Mountains west of Sydney. I recall images of old looking engines (turn of the century 2–8–0s) assisting very much bigger and newer ones (3 cylinder 4–8–2s). They slogged up the severe grades to Katoomba, smoke rising skywards and the sound of their exertions echoing out of cuttings and across valleys.

Other holidays were spent north of Sydney. Driving to the Central Coast in summer, at that time, meant sitting in a traffic jam for long spells near the Hawkesbury River. A constant procession of trains, many double headed, battling their way up Cowan Bank's 1 in 40 made such delays quite entertaining.

Electrification had draped its metallic shroud over both stretches of railway by the early 1960s. But there were plenty of steam locos working elsewhere and by now I was in secondary school and had made friends with other enthusiasts. I acquired my first camera in 1964, by which time an inherited travel bug was already dragging me around the state on weekends and during school holidays.

New South Wales country centres were then linked to Sydney by mail trains. These left the city in the evening and reached their destinations sometime next day. As a schoolboy, of course, I was unable to afford a sleeping berth, but the sitting cars were of side corridor design, so sleeping bags would be spread out in an empty compartment. If the train was full there were always luggage racks which could be padded with clothing and made quite comfortable. Other passengers were usually happy with the arrangement as it created more room on the seats. By the small hours of the morning the train would be far from the city.

Ingham, Queensland 1976

The night view from the carriage window was moonlit silver touching a vast unknowable blackness, edged by the flickering gold glow from an open firebox door.

Weekends were opportunities to combine my love of camping with train photography. My favourite venue was Hawkmount, a forest covered ridge on the busy Sydney to Newcastle main line. One could take a tent or avail oneself of the dubious comforts of a lineside fettlers' hut known to many as the Hawkmount Hotel. On still winter nights northbound trains were audible as they accelerated along the level before tackling the grade. The frenetic staccato became louder and more laboured as the 1 in 40 retarded momentum. In a crescendo of crashing exhaust and clanking rods the locos roared past the hut, cylinders only feet from the recumbent bodies within. The heaviest freights were Garratt-hauled. The exhausts from their two engine units produced a fascinating rhythm as they resonated in and out of synchronisation, contrary to suggestions in the British railfan press at the time.

As well as these 4–8–4+4–8–4 Garratts, six other classes of steam loco worked over Hawkmount in the 1960s. Sprightly 4–6–0s on stopping passenger trains, speedy Pacifics on expresses, veteran 2–8–0s and newer, light 2–8–2s on freights. All classes could turn up in any double header combination on north bound trains. With the transfer of more Garratts to Broadmeadow (Newcastle) shed in the late 1960s, double headed Garratts became common. 520 tons of locomotive with 8 cylinders and over 126,000 pounds of combined tractive effort produced an awesome display on the 1 in 44 grades, especially if rails were wet and the load had been optimistically increased beyond the rated limit.

New South Wales, of course, was not the only steamy state. Australian state governments developed their railway systems on different gauges, displaying the sort of administrative myopia which continues to earn them condemnation today. It has to be said, however, that such ineptitude created a paradise for railway enthusiasts. In one country we had seven major railway systems plus dozens of industrial lines using five different gauges. The six state government systems, as well as many of the private ones, had developed their own loco designs and operating ideas.

Many of these amazingly numerous loco types worked infrequently on remote country branch lines. A car was needed to capture such workings on film and even to get to otherwise inaccessible locations on many busy lines. Several carloads of fans would often get together especially for events like the end of steam on the South Australian narrow gauge. The word 'cade' (verb and noun), abbreviation of 'motorcade', entered railfan vocabulary in the 1960s to describe the strange spectacle of several teams of maniacs driving beside a train at speed in a cloud of dust.

A camaraderie developed at such times. Lunch at a pub and dinner around the campfire were social events at which enthusiasts from interstate and even overseas congregated, swapped news and began friendships. During one such get together in Western Australia, I became involved in a discussion on the relative merits of New South Wales and East African Garratts. To emphasise my point, I invoked the name of British author A. E. Durrant, whose definitive book on Garratts had appeared a couple of years earlier. To my surprise the person sitting next to me turned out to be none other than A. E. (Dusty) Durrant.

While I was at school my parents viewed my frequent weekend absences with understandable despair. They were more aware of exam timetables than I was. A failed first attempt at university showed that they were right, but my consequent acquisition of employment provided funds for travel beyond Australia's shores.

By the early 70s Australia as a railfan haunt had become very limited. Most of the rest of the world was still very steamy so it was time to look further afield. I began with a brief visit to New Zealand in 1970, but my first truly foreign bash was to South East Asia in 1972. The final two weeks of the trip were spent in Indonesia, then a cornucopia of steam loco variety. As well as 2-4-0s, 2 cylinder compound 4-4-0s and steam trams, there were 0-4-0 tender locos reminiscent of old Hornby wind-up O gauge locos.

The Indonesian environment was totally different from Australia's. Passengers shared carriage space with domestic animals and village halts were a mass of people, colour and noise. In the mountains of Java large Mallets still twisted their cumbersome double drive units around tortuous bends on grades as steep as 1 in 20. One such line, from Tjibatu to Tjikadjang, skirted the rugged slopes of volcanic Mount Galunggung, providing a last habitat for CC50 Class 2-6-6-0s. The steeply terraced paddy fields were sufficiently high to escape Asia's pervasive tropical haze layer and the light was delightfully crisp. In 1980 the area was devastated by a major eruption.

Travelling with friends was far preferable to going it alone. In the late 60s I had met a fellow Sydneysider, Malcolm Holdsworth and a few years later, in South Africa, I was introduced to a young fan just arrived from Melbourne, named George Bambery. Over the years the three of us became a team. We conceived this book in the mid 1970s. That it should have taken almost 20 years to become reality is fitting. Our individual photographic styles have developed during that time and our collections have become sufficiently diverse to allow representative selections.

Train photography in Southern Africa in the early and mid 70s was as easy and relaxed as it had been at home. Nights were usually spent under the stars after grilling succulent steaks over the campfire and imbibing smooth Cape red wine. Not only were we treated to a night long steam symphony but we would be on the spot at dawn for those soft golden first rays and, if a train turned up at the same moment, the best photos of the day. The middle of the day, when light turned to glare and the heat was enervating, was spent at the beach, in a pub or dozing under a tree. Cading resumed for the late afternoon light.

South Africa, despite its 3′ 6″ gauge tracks, had locos as big as New South Wales' biggest, hauling heavier, more frequent trains at greater speeds. The Kroonstad–Bloemfontein main line, for example, with 120 trains per day, was busier than any Australian inter-city line. It was entirely steam worked by heavy 4-8-2s of the 15F and 23 Classes. Performances of the great 25NC Class 4-8-4s on Kimberley–De Aar were outstanding. As late as 1991 they could still be seen hauling 18 car expresses at speeds in excess of 125 kph. In this context one wonders why 4′ 8½″ was chosen as Australia's standard gauge.

Much of Africa was Garratt territory. The mighty maroon 59s worked most of the freight from the steamy Indian Ocean port of Mombasa to Kenya's capital, Nairobi, 500km inland and 1700m above sea level. To me, the world's most elegant Garratts are the Zimbabwean 15th Class 4-6-4+4-6-4s. Equally competent on express passenger or freight, they are brilliant performers.

The quintessential African sound was heard in the bush at dusk when the air was still and wild animals were growling, coughing, howling. A distant melodious whistle preceded a few slow barks which quickened to a distinctive Garratt stutter as another freight got away from a lonely watering stop. I always enjoy photting well away from main roads and habitation, preferably on the roughest lineside access tracks. A couple of years ago we witnessed a scene like this in Zimbabwe. The bush felt and looked much like the Australian scrub country and the Garratt sounds could certainly have been in Queensland or South Australia. Next morning, however, a friend photographed a train at the same spot and came face to face with a lioness after pressing the shutter. Similarities were suddenly irrelevant.

Clearly camping in lion country was not an option. But near the Zimbabwean town of Hwange is the Baobab Hotel. Situated on a hilltop above the railway line, the Baobab was an ideal base for steam enthusiasts. The recently retired manageress, Norma Hammond, actively encouraged her 'rail nuts' and made them feel very welcome. Similar hospitality at hotels around the world has contributed to the success of many trips.

The availability of self drive rental cars in most countries has proved invaluable. We have had to contend with a range of driving conditions. Once we drove into a mud slide as it oozed our VW closer and closer towards the edge of a several thousand foot precipice high in the Ecuadorian Andes and there have been many challenging encounters with blizzards in Turkey. Familiarity, however, does not necessarily breed expertise. Black ice once proved our undoing in far southern Argentina, when our rented Peugeot spun out of control and flipped over. Fortunately none of us was injured and the dealer showed great presence of mind by offering us another car!

My favourite part of the world is Patagonia, that empty wilderness of rocky plains and the hauntingly beautiful Andes at the southern tip of South America. The world's most southerly railway hauls coal from an isolated mine in the Andean foothills across the 300km breadth of the continent, at that point, to the port of Rio Gallegos on the Atlantic coast. Despite a gauge of 750mm, trains in excess of 1,200 tonnes are hauled by modern stoker fired 2-10-2s.

Strangely the line has been largely avoided by enthusiasts despite the excellent light quality found so far from the equator and wild scenery peppered with extinct mini volcanos. In winter blizzards often close the road, the temperature can drop to −20 degrees and the river freezes over. But sunrise and sunset skies remain charged with colour for over an hour and the sun skims the horizon all day with wonderful photographic consequences. Superb Argentine asados and home-made chorizo sausages, supplemented for special guests with huge brown trout (caught in the season, of course), are served by Orlando and Rolando Van Heerden beside the fire at the remote Bella Vista Hotel. Train drivers chime a deep steamboat whistle greeting as they rumble past just outside the door.

Occasionally we have found ourselves caught up in major world events. It happened in Patagonia in March 1982. Heavy military activity in the form of army patrols and airforce over-flights were increasing from day to day. This was a worrying development as many people had been known to disappear at the hands of the then brutal Argentine military regime. We facetiously wondered if Argentina were preparing to invade the Falklands/Malvinas Islands. Four weeks later they did!

Sadly, with the passage of time, few of the photos can be repeated. I wish to conclude by questioning the decision of many railway systems to eliminate steam. Many countries have ample coal reserves but no domestic oil. Foreign exchange is squandered importing oil while local coal miners lose their jobs. Frequently the steam locos replaced are perfectly capable of hauling their systems' freight and passengers for many years into the future. Often the diesels that replace them haul smaller loads at lower speeds. Who gains from this arrangement?

Australia, February 1966 *A hundred and ninety one and a half miles from Sydney Terminal Station, number 63 Mudgee Mail has arrived at its destination behind Ten Wheeler 3387.*

Australia, May 1972 Coal is the major traffic on the four track main line into Newcastle from Maitland, New South Wales. The venerable 53 Class 2–8–0 clanking its ageing wheels up Thornton Bank was just one in a procession of unbraked trains.

Australia, February 1971 CCS 23, a rebuilt Beyer
Peacock 2–6–0, rests in Tasmania's Launceston shed
between duties on railway centenary specials.

Australia, November 1970 In World War I the Railway Operating Division of the British Army chose the design of the Great Central Railway's versatile 04 Class for locomotives to be used on the Western Front. After the war a number of these aesthetically pleasing 2–8–0s came to Australia for duties on the private railways serving John Brown's coal empire. No. 23's English lines do not look too out of place as it climbs away from Stockrington Colliery.

South Africa, July 1974 South African Railways effectively ran standard gauge locos on narrow gauge tracks. A 23 Class heavy 4–8–2 rumbles across the bridge at Glen with freight for Bloemfontein.

Australia, December 1969 South Australia's 3'6" gauge 400 Class Garratts had been withdrawn early in the 1960s. As main line conversion to standard gauge approached, diesels were taken out of service for regauging, but Broken Hill's valuable ore had to reach the coast, so the Garratts were thrown back into the fray. The sun has already set at Caltowie as No. 402 blasts eastwards towards home base at Peterborough.

Portugal, December 1975 Trains on the 106 kilometre long metre gauge Tua line steamed straight out of the 19th century. An elderly 2–6–0T climbs into the hills with the morning mixed from Mirandela to Bragança.

Portugal, December 1975 Régua shed in the Douro Valley's picturesque port wine growing area served two gauges (5'6" and metre) and a variety of locos. On the broad gauge roads a 2–6–4T, with only blast spreading chimney visible, has just worked in from Porto while an outside cylinder 4–6–0 swivels on the turntable prior to working up to the Spanish border. Another 4–6–0 awaits fresh duties. A stud of 2–4–6–0 Mallet tanks provides power for the heavily graded metre gauge Corgo branch.

Australia, July 1977 Steam on the South Maitland Railways in New South Wales survived until 1983. In 1977 coal was still carried in non air braked wooden four wheeled hoppers. A Beyer Peacock 2–8–2 tank climbs away from East Greta Junction on a cold winter's morning.

▲ Syria, January 1976
A Swiss built 2–6–0 tank on a train from Damascus to the Lebanese border climbs through the Baraba Gorge, scene of fighting in World War 2 involving Australian troops. Driving out of Damascus a few hours before taking this photo, we found ourselves in the middle of a huge military convoy heading west. It was the Syrian Army on its way to invade Lebanon.

◀ Syria, January 1976
Driver of SLM-built 1050mm gauge 2–6–0 tank, Damascus.

Turkey, January 1976 'Skyliner' on the march between
Sumuçak and Kurşunlu on the Zonguldak line.

Turkey, January 1976 The 'Skyliner' 2–10–0s at each end of this heavy freight are in full cry, building up momentum for the long, icy climb to Çankiri.

▲ **Kenya, November 1977** Late afternoon in Tsavo
National Park. Metre gauge Garratt 6007, formerly named
Sir Mark Young, rolls the mixed from Taveta to Voi.

◀ **Kenya, November 1977** A 59 Class pits its mammoth
89,000 lbs tractive effort against the grade and its load of box
cars as it stamps into Kiu on the Mombasa–Nairobi main line.

Jugoslavia, December 1977
The four cylindered 01 Class 2–6–2s, formerly of the Serbian State Railways, were beautiful locos. Here one makes heavy weather of the climb into the mountains of troubled Kosovo Province with a Niš to Priština passenger. Who left the bloody door open?

Austria, December 1977 All thoughts of an early start for the long drive back to Munich were forgotten when the sky finally cleared after several days of bad weather. The village streets echo to the roar of compound cylinders and grinding rack cogs as a pair of ancient 97 Class 0–6–2Ts lift a train of empties out of Vordernberg yard.

South Africa, August 1978 Rosmead Station, in Cape
Province, briefly comes to life as an East London train arrives
from the north and swaps its diesels for a pair of 15AR Class
4–8–2s. Soon the sleeping passengers will be continuing their
long journey through the winter night and Rosmead will slip
back into hibernation.

South Africa, August 1978 The 19D and 15AR Class
4–8–2s on this west bound train on the Stormberg to
Rosmead line are in a hurry. Steam will not be cut off for the
brief water stop at Schoombee until the last possible moment.

Poland, November 1974 Train photography in Poland
was a risky business. Fortunately the lineside lake near Brody
on the Rozwadów–Lódź line was out of the way so no-one
in authority saw this photo taken. A Pt47 Class 2–8–2
steams northwards on an express.

India, December 1982 At dawn on Chilka Lake, the canoes are setting out for the day's fishing and a WG Class broad gauge heavy 2–8–2 ambles past the fish traps with an east coast passenger.

▲ **Indonesia, August 1979** By the late 1970s Indonesia was the last haunt of large Mallets. A 2–6–6–0 of the CC50 Class climbs into the clear mountain air of central Java with an afternoon train from Tjibatu to Tjikadjang.

◄ **Indonesia, August 1979** The Buddhist cupolas of Borobudur rest in a Muslim land.

Indonesia, August 1979 0–4–0 tank locos were common around the world but who ever heard of an 0–4–0 tender design? The Indonesian State Railways B52 Class were just such exotic specimens and, in 1979, still worked the Tegal–Prupuk line. B5212 with the morning train from Prupuk arrives at a village amid the usual crush of rural humanity.

Brazil, December 1977 The newest loco on the 750mm gauge São João del Rei system was built by Baldwin in 1919. The oil fire of 2–8–0 No. 68 casts a glow over the burnt-out shell of the old roundhouse.

Chile, February 1982 Lines branching off the 5'6" gauge main trunk penetrate some of the dark, forested valleys in the south of Chile. The deep whistle of an Alco-built 70 Class 2–8–2 shatters the rustic tranquility as it leaves Malalcuello with the morning train from Lonquimay back to Victoria. A 4.5km long combined rail/road tunnel through the Andes is a feature of this line.

Chile, January 1978 Handsome 80 Class 4–8–2 number 860 spent half an hour at Afquintue waiting for two opposing movements. During that time we were invited into the cab for afternoon tea. Finally the 'right of way' was given so, with whistle chiming and bell ringing, 860 eased her heavy Temuco to Osorno freight out of the station precincts.

East Germany, May 1980 In 1980 both the
Berlin Wall and the Iron Curtain were in place
and the red flags still fluttered over the eastern
part of Germany. Deutsche Reichsbahn 03.10
Class Pacifics, however, were in their last month
of service on the Berlin–Stralsund expresses.
This did not affect their performance. Heralded
by an urgent 3 cylinder howl, 03.0010 storms
northwards near Chorin at about 130kph, leaving
a hurricane force slipstream in its wake.

Poland, April 1980 In Poland, as in other communist
countries, railway photography from a main road was
inadvisable. At roadside picnic places, however, parked cars
were less likely to attract police attention and possible
arrest. Of course this Tkt 48 Class 2–8–2 tank just happened
to rumble across this photogenic viaduct with the morning
passenger from Kudowa Zdrój to Kłodzko while we were
innocently having breakfast.

India, December 1983 The train from Darjeeling climbs past Batasia to the line's summit at Ghum, elevation 2,242 metres. Roughly 90 kms away Kanchenjunga, the world's third highest peak, looms at 8,535 metres.

India, January 1981 A YP hurries an evening suburban
train out of Secunderabad. A light engine from the loco shed
steams towards the station to work another rush hour
passenger service. Don't be fooled into thinking that the
paintwork on the carriages is two-toned. The bottom half is
clinging commuters!

India, December 1983 An Indian Railways YP Class
metre gauge 4–6–2 prepares to leave busy Secunderabad
Station with a night train.

Pakistan, January 1984
An elegant XA Class light Pacific
starts the morning Multan train
from Kundian amid local
Pakistani colour.

Pakistan, January 1984 An HGS Class 2–8–0 comes off shed at Quetta to work the daily train over the Kojak Pass to the Afghan border.

Pakistan, January 1983 Any aspiring invader in southern Asia knows that the Khyber Pass is the way to go. Alexander the Great went that way when he invaded India over 2,200 years ago and the British used it in the other direction when they moved into Afghanistan late last century. The Brits lost, but built a railway up the pass anyway. This Pakistan Railways train is up the Khyber in more ways than one as the lead SGS Class inside cylinder 0–6–0 has broken a connecting rod. Friendly locals investigate.

Turkey, December 1981 Turkey and Iran share a common railway gauge and their systems meet at the frontier, but traffic on the Turkish side must traverse Lake Van first. A 'Middle Easter' 2–8–2 shunts wagons onto a train ferry at Tatvan, the port at the western end of the lake.

▲ **India, January 1981** On India's metre gauge, a YG Class 2–8–2 leaves Nanjangud with an evening stopper for Mysore.

▶ **Australia, September 1981** Steam on the New South Wales Government Railways finished in 1973, but several locos were retained for special workings. 59 Class 2–8–2 No. 5917 is captured on a fan trip between Narromine and Dubbo. A couple of minutes after the train passed the sun set, the campfire was lit and the red wine was opened.

Ecuador, January 1982 At Bucay the Guayaquil and Quito
Railway starts climbing the Andes. This large 2–8–0 is about
to take the train on to Riobamba after replacing a 2–6–0.
It is a long haul, involving a climb of about 3,500 metres to
Palmira, but the crew does not intend to go hungry.

▲ **India, December 1982** The morning train from Ooty to Coonor, in the Nilgiri Hills of southern India, descends towards the cloud layer. Motive power on the metre gauge line is exclusively X Class 0–8–2 rack and adhesion tanks.

◄ **India, December 1992** Ten years later the timetable had changed. The first working of the morning now ran from Coonor to Ooty. An X Class eases onto its cars at Coonor just after dawn.

Brazil, June 1985 Although only metre gauge, the American
built 2–10–4s of Brazil's Dona Teresa Cristina system were
impressive beasts. The ground shook as this one lifted a string
of empty coal wagons towards Sideropolis tunnel on the Rio
Fiorita branch.

Argentina, July 1989 The 750mm gauge
Esquel Branch in Patagonia is a line of long grades
and dramatic mountain scenery. An outside-
framed Baldwin 2–8–2 climbs out of the Rio
Chico valley. The Andean foothills form a
rampart along the horizon.

Argentina, July 1992 With 1,200 tonnes of coal in tow a
750mm gauge 2–10–2 slogs it out on the approach to La Sofia
as night spreads over the Rio Gallegos.

Turkey, December 1981 A 'Skyliner' 2–10–0 stamps southwards into the night with a freight for Ulukişla from Kayseri.

Germany, January 1993 Mid-winter dawn at Stiege
in the Harz. Simultaneous departure.

Argentina, July 1989 A heavy Patagonian sky threatens to dump more snow as a Hitachi 2–10–2 rolls westwards near Capitan Eyroa.

▲ **Zimbabwe, July 1993** Dawn at Bulawayo shed. 15th and
16th Class Garratts soak up the early rays.

◄ **Zimbabwe, July 1991** The long climb from Hwange to
Dete on the Victoria Falls line required a major effort from
locos and their crews. This 15th Class double 4–6–4 between
Lukosi and Pongoro had maximum tonnage and an
enthusiastic fireman.

China, January 1992 The frantic jackhammer exhaust
could be heard for half an hour through clear, superchilled air
as a pass link QJ made up for lost time on the 1 in 80 climb
out of the Yellow River Valley. Men Jia Wan. Train No. 43
Lanzhou Express.

China, December 1991 A photo of a pair of ice sheathed QJ Class 2–10–2s blasting out of a Gobi Desert dawn cannot convey the pain of frozen toes, the numbness of inoperable fingers, nor the prickle as breath solidifies on the face in a 30 degree below zero wind. Men Jia Wan.

China, December 1992 A QJ 2–10–2 recedes into
the haze with a light freight near Hexipu.
(George Bambery)